Mother Teresa
A SYMBOL OF KINDNESS

An Imprint of Om Books International

Published in 2014 by

OM
KIDZ

An imprint of Om Books International

Corporate & Editorial Office
A 12, Sector 64, Noida 201 301
Uttar Pradesh, India
Phone: +91 120 477 4100
Email: editorial@ombooks.com
Website: www.ombooksinternational.com

Sales Office
4379/4B, Prakash House, Ansari Road
Darya Ganj, New Delhi 110 002, India
Phone: +91 11 2326 3363, 2326 5303
Fax: +91 11 2327 8091
Email: sales@ombooks.com
Website: www.ombooks.com

Content by Shubhojit Sanyal
Illustrations: Aadil Khan, Naushad Ali, Himanshu Sharma

ISBN : 978-93-82607-68-7

Printed at EIH Press, Gurgaon, India

10 9 8 7 6 5 4 3 2 1

Contents

Birth

Mother Teresa as she's famously known was born on 26 August 1910 in Skopje, the current capital of the Republic of Macedonia (her date of birth is disputed). She was baptised as Agnes Gonxha Bojaxhiu. Her parents, Nikola and Drana Bojaxhiu, were of Albanian descent. Her father was an entrepreneur and was deeply involved in politics advocating the independence of Albanians. It was a devoutly Catholic family. Agnes had an older brother and an older sister.

Early Life

Agnes was around 8 years old when her father suddenly fell ill and died. While the cause of his death remained unknown, many speculated that political enemies poisoned him. After his death, Agnes became extraordinarily close to her mother, a pious and compassionate woman who instilled in her daughter a deep commitment to charity.

After Nikola's death the family lost all its riches. But this did not stop Drana Bojaxhiu to extend an open invitation to destitutes to dine with her family at their home on a regular basis. Thus Drana instilled the values of sharing and caring in her children from a very tender age.

Religious Calling

Agnes attended a convent-run primary school and then a state-run secondary school. As a girl, Agnes sang in the local Sacred Heart choir. Her religious formation was further assisted by the vibrant Jesuit parish of the Sacred Heart in which she was much involved. At the age of 12, Agnes first felt a calling to a religious life. She often heard about the missionaries working in India and was drawn towards them.

In 1928, an 18-year-old Agnes decided to become a nun and set off for Ireland to join the Institute of the Blessed Virgin Mary (known as the Sisters of Loreto) in Ireland. There she received the name Sister Mary Teresa.

A few months later she left for India, and arrived in Calcutta (now called Kolkata) in January 1929. After two years, she took her vows on 24 May.

Sister Teresa Life as a Teacher

Sister Teresa began teaching at the Saint Mary's High School for Girls in Calcutta run by the Loreto Sisters and dedicated to teaching girls from the city's poorest families. Sister Teresa learned to speak Bengali and Hindi fluently, and was an outstanding teacher.

On 24 May 1937, she took her final vows and henceforth was called Mother Teresa.

She continued to teach at Saint Mary's and in 1944 she became the school's principal.

A New Calling

Mother Teresa had been teaching for many years but she wasn't oblivious to the conditions outside in the city–the riots, Indian Freedom Movement and The Great Famine of Bengal (1943).

On 10 September 1946, Mother Teresa experienced a second calling that transformed her life forever. She was on a train from Calcutta to Darjeeling when Jesus Christ spoke to her and told her to abandon teaching and work for the poorest and sickest people.

As Mother Teresa had taken a vow of obedience, she could not leave her convent without official permission. Finally in January 1948, she received approval from the local Archbishop Ferdinand Périer to pursue this new calling.

In Service of the Poor

In the August of 1948, Mother Teresa abandoned her sheltered life of the convent and started wearing the white saree with a blue border, which she would always wear in public for the rest of her life.

After a short course with the Medical Mission Sisters in Patna, Mother Teresa returned to Calcutta and found temporary lodging with the Little Sisters of the Poor. In December 1948, she visited the Calcutta's slums to serve the poor.

Mother Teresa quickly translated her calling into concrete actions to help the city's poor. She founded an open air school where she taught children by making drawings on mud with a stick, as she had no slates, blackboards and other infrastructure.

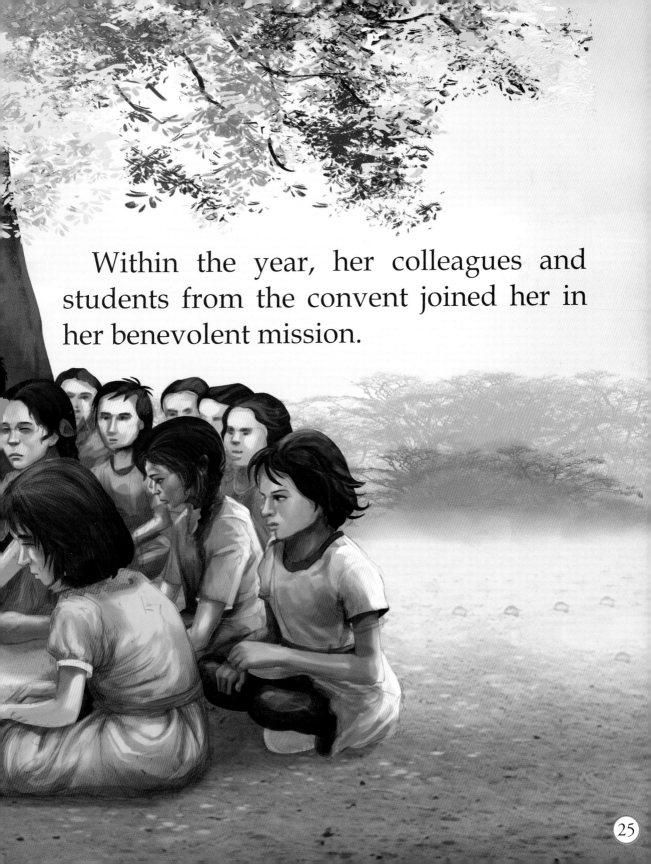

Within the year, her colleagues and students from the convent joined her in her benevolent mission.

Overcoming Despair and Doubt

As Mother Teresa began her work to help the poor, she was often short on funds and would often have to beg for food and medical supplies and many a times met with disappointment. However, it was only her love for Jesus Christ that she continued to work with the poor, feeding them, educating them and looking after them.

In October 1950, she received permission from the Holy See to start a new order, The Missionaries of Charity, which she founded with only twelve members; most of them were former teachers or pupils from St. Mary's School. Its mission was to care for the hungry, the naked, the homeless, the crippled, the blind, the lepers, all those people who feel unwanted, unloved, uncared for throughout society; people who have become a burden to the society and are shunned by everyone.

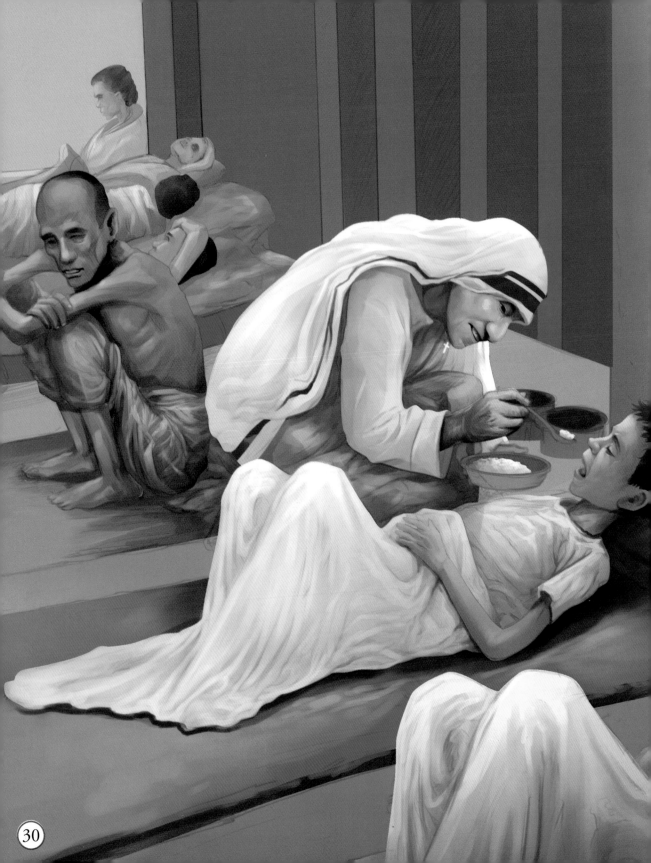

Mother to the Needy

One thing that greatly troubled Mother Teresa was the way in which the poor, homeless and diseased were left to rot to their deaths on the streets of Calcutta. According to her, "loneliness and the feeling of being unwanted was the greatest poverty."

In 1952, she established the free hospice Nirmal Hriday (Home for the Pure of Heart).

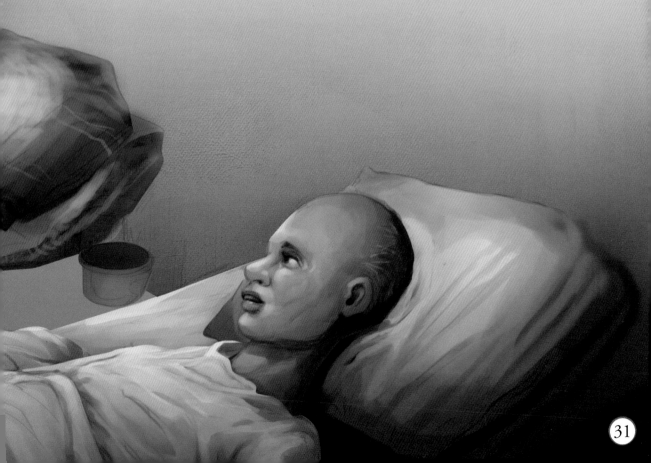

Here the poor, destitute and diseased souls from the streets, were washed and cleaned and given space so that they could die a dignified death. After their death they were cremated according to their religion.

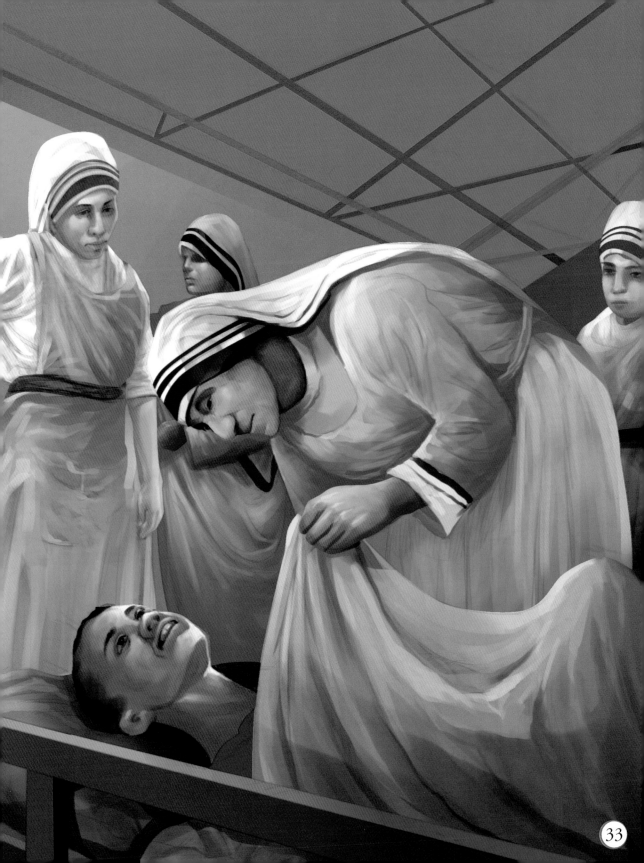

A Beacon of Hope and Love

Mother Teresa's work was not done just yet. Shortly after establishing Nirmal Hriday, she realised that the city had a huge population of lepers who were shunned by people because of their disease. The Missionaries of Charity then started a colony for the lepers called Shanti Nagar (Town of Peace) near Asansol.

The Missionaries of Charity even established several outposts and clinics, where lepers could be provided basic medical facilities and care.

Mother Teresa established the Nirmala Shishu Bhavan in 1955, a place to house homeless children and orphans who roamed the city streets and slums of Calcutta.

The work by Mother Teresa and her Missionaries of Charity soon started to attract the attention of people from all over the world. The Indian government too worked with her in securing buildings for her, where she could carry out her work for the poor and downtrodden. Several wealthy humanitarians also contributed to her mission.

By 1960, the Missionaries of Charity celebrated its 10th anniversary and were given permission to establish houses outside of Calcutta, but within India. Almost immediately, houses were established in Delhi, Ranchi and Jhansi; more followed soon.

International Charity

For their 15th anniversary, Pope John Paul VI gave permission to the Missionaries of Charity to establish houses outside India. Mother Teresa's fluency in several languages greatly helped her when she went abroad to raise funds for her mission. She attached great importance to her ability to communicate and connect with people to carry out her work.

The first Missionaries of Charity branch was esablished in Venezuela. It was soon followed by foundations in Rome and Tanzania and eventually on every continent.

By 1963, Mother Teresa had also established the Missionaries of Charity Brothers in Calcutta, enabling men to also join her in her endeavours to bring peace and happiness in the world. By 2013, their presence was in 21 countries.

She even established several non-Catholic organisations which all worked towards helping the poor and destitutes.

In 1971, Mother Teresa travelled to New York where she opened a soup kitchen as well as a home to care for those suffering from AIDS.

A Symbol of Peace and Understanding

Mother Teresa worked intensely to bring peace and stability to the world. For example, in 1982, near the end of the Siege of Beirut, she rescued 37 children trapped in a burning hospital by creating a momentary ceasefire between Palestinian guerillas and the Israeli army. She travelled across the war zone alongside Red Cross workers to bring the children to safety.

Mother Teresa even visited Armenia during the aftermath of the 1988 Spitak earthquake. She, along with her sisters, worked tirelessly in rescuing trapped survivors and providing food and medical relief.

Mother Teresa also served for a long time in Ethiopia, bringing food and supplies to the starving nation. One of her landmark missions

was to Chernobyl in Ukraine in 1986, where she worked extensively with people exposed to nuclear radiation from a nearby nuclear plant explosion.

Awards and Achievements

Mother Teresa received many awards in her lifetime; this chapter lists a few major ones. In 1962, the Indian Government recognised the generous contributions of Mother Teresa towards the betterment of society and awarded her the Padma Shri, one of its highest civilian honours.

In 1962, Mother Teresa received the prestigious Ramon Magsaysay Award for International Understanding from the Philippines Government.

In 1979, Mother Teresa was awarded the Nobel Peace Prize for work undertaken to overcome poverty and distress, which also constitutes a threat to peace. But true to her nature, Mother Teresa asked the Nobel committee to donate her prize money to the poor.

In 1980, the Indian Government conferred her with the Bharat Ratna, the country's highest civilian award.

Finally in 1994, her country of origin, Albania, conferred on her the highest civilian award of the state, the Golden Honour of the Nation.

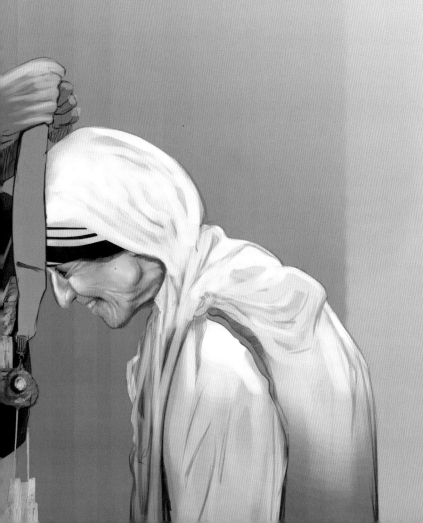

In 1982, she was appointed as the honorary companion of the Order of Australia. It is one of the highest awards for Australian civilians, also given to non-Australians of exceptional merit.

In 1983, Mother Teresa was awarded the Order of Merit by the British Government for her humanitarian work. Two years later, the United States Government awarded her with the Presidential Medal for Freedom.

Ultimate Unification with the Lord

Mother Teresa's health started failing from 1983, when she suffered from her first heart attack when visiting Pope John Paul II in Rome. However, she refused to slow down and in 1989, she had a second heart attack. She was provided with an artificial pacemaker. But shortly after, in 1991, Mother Teresa fell severely ill with pneumonia while she was visiting Mexico.

Again in August 1996, Mother Teresa suffered from an attack of malaria, which not only left her very weak and vulnerable, but also affected her ailing heart greatly.

Mother Teresa finally resigned from the Missionaries of Charity on 13 March 1997 due to her failing health. She died on 5 September in the same year. From having started out alone in her humanitarian endeavours, Mother Teresa left the world with over 4, 000 sisters of the Missionaries of Charity in nearly 120 countries.

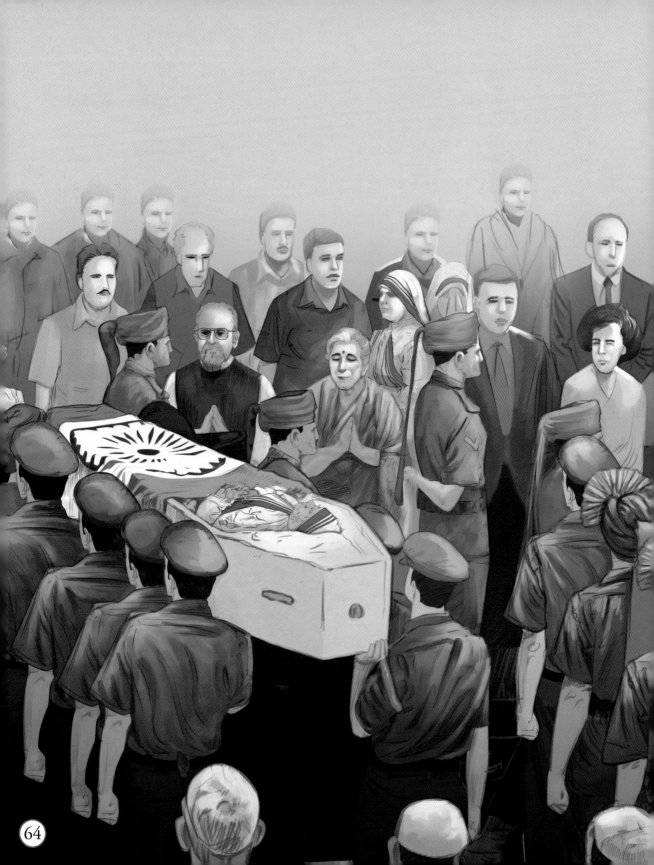

The Indian Government gave her a state funeral in recognition and gratitude for her hard work and humanitarian efforts. Her death was condoned by all heads of state, including the former UN Secretary General Javier Pérez de Cuéllar paying her the highest compliment by saying, "Mother Teresa is the United Nations. Mother Teresa is peace in the world."

Blessed Teresa of Calcutta

The Catholic world had often bestowed several awards on Mother Teresa for carrying out the Lord's work. In 1971, Pope Paul VI conferred on her the Pope John XXIII Peace Prize for her work with the poor.

Pope John Paul II began the process for her canonisation; the steps required before acknowledging her as a saint. However, before she could be canonised, the Vatican doctrine stated that she would have to perform a miracle after her death to prove her divine powers.

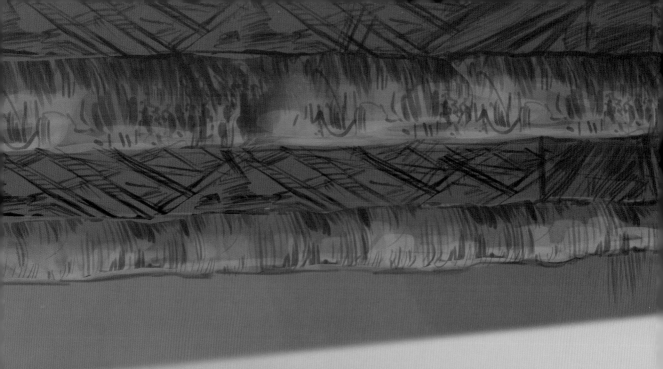

Finally one of Mother Teresa's devotees, Monica Besra, declared that she had been suffering from a malignant tumour and one night, a beam of light emitted from a picture of Mother Teresa. She prayed for Mother Teresa to come to her aid and the next day, the doctor's declared her to be free from any ailment.

That healing occurred on the first anniversary of Mother Teresa's death.

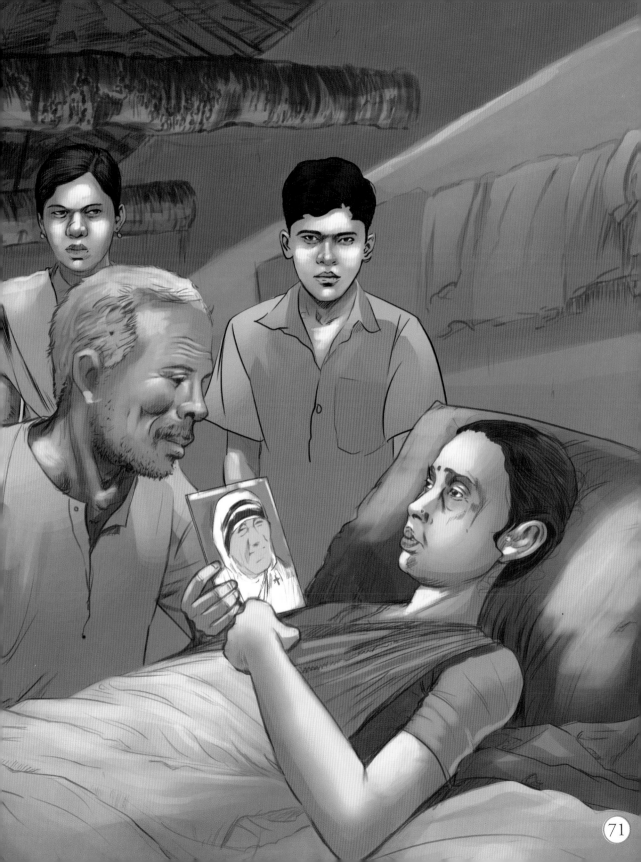

While there are several critical views on this, the Holy Father finally agreed to accept this as a miracle in 2002, and Mother Teresa was beatified by Pope John Paul II at Vatican City on 19 October 2003, earning her the title of "Blessed" Teresa of Calcutta.

After her beatification, the recognition of another miracle will be required for sainthood.

The Final Resting Place

Mother Teresa is buried on the ground floor of the Mother House of the Missionaries of Charity, Kolkata. Her tomb has become a place of pilgrimage and quiet meditation for people of all creeds around the world.

Mother Teresa

USA 44

2010

In Praise of Mother Teresa

Known as the "Saint of the Gutters", Mother Teresa inspired admiration and devotion from people all over the world. On her 100th birth anniversary, Pope Benedict XVI observed in a special message, "This year will be for the Church and the world an occasion of joyful gratitude to God for the inestimable gift that Mother Teresa was in her lifetime and continues to be through the affectionate and tireless work of you, her spiritual children."

On 5 September 2010, The U S Postal Service issued a commemorative postage stamp in appreciation of Mother Teresa.

Many renowned personalities have praised Mother Teresa. A couple of such thoughts are shared hereunder:

"She leaves us a strong message, which has no borders and which goes beyond faith: helping, listening, solidarity," former French President Jacques Chirac.

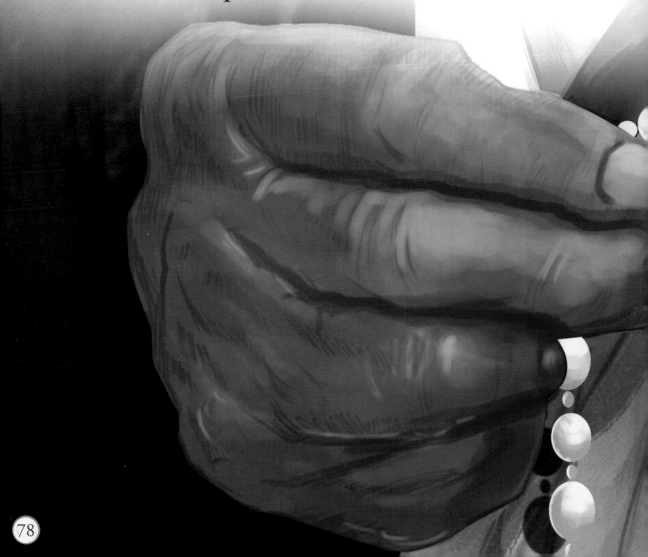

"A loss to the entire humanity. She will be deeply missed in our efforts to build international peace, and a just, caring and equitable world order," Late South African President Nelson Mandela.

TITLES IN THIS SERIES

  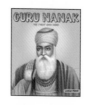 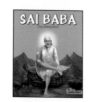